CHILDREN AND THEIR MOTHERS

A *terra magica* BOOK

To Suzanne

HANNS REICH

Children and Their Mothers

With Love,
Jeni

HILL AND WANG • NEW YORK

A division of Farrar, Straus and Giroux

Copyright © 1964 by Hanns Reich Verlag
(now Reich Verlag AG, Lucerne, Switzerland)
All rights reserved
Printed in the United States of America
Published in Canada by Collins Publishers
Library of Congress catalog card number: 64-24833
ISBN: 0-8090-1513-7

Women know
The way to rear up children (to be just),
They know a simple, merry tender knack
Of tying sashes, fitting baby-shoes,
And stringing pretty words that make no sense,
And kissing full sense into empty words,
Which things are corals to cut life upon,
Although such trifles; children learn by such
Love's holy earnest in a pretty play
And get not over early solemnized,
But seeing, as in a rose-bush, Love's Divine
Which burns and hurts not,—not a single bloom,—
Become aware and unafraid of Love.
Such good do mothers.

Elizabeth Barrett Browning
(from Aurora Leigh)

SHE WAS A PHANTOM OF DELIGHT

She was a phantom of delight
When first she gleamed upon my sight;
A lovely apparition, sent
To be a moment's ornament;
Her eyes as stars of twilight fair;
Like twilight's, too, her dusky hair;
But all things else about her drawn
From May-time and the cheerful dawn;
A dancing shape, an image gay,
To haunt, to startle, and waylay.

I saw her upon nearer view,
A spirit yet a Woman too!
Her household motions light and free
And steps of virgin-liberty;
A countenance in which did meet
Sweet records, promises as sweet;
A creature not too bright or good
For human nature's daily food,
For transient sorrows, simple wiles,
Praise, blame, love, kisses, tears and smiles.

And now I see with eye serene
The very pulse of the machine;
A being breathing thoughtful breath,
A traveller between life and death:
The reason firm, the temperate will,
Endurance, foresight, strength, and skill;
A perfect Woman, nobly planned
To warn, to comfort, and command;
And yet a Spirit still, and bright
With something of an angel-light.

William Wordsworth

THE JUDGMENT OF SOLOMON

Then came there two women that were harlots, unto the king, and stood before him.

And the one woman said, O my lord, I and this woman dwell in one house; and I was delivered of a child with her in the house.

And it came to pass the third day after that I was delivered, that this woman was delivered also: and we were together; there was no stranger with us.

And this woman's child died in the night; because she overlaid it.

And she arose at midnight, and took my son from beside me, while thine handmaiden slept, and laid it in her bosom, and laid her dead child in my bosom.

And when I rose in the morning to give my child suck, behold, it was dead: but when I had considered it in the morning, behold, it was not my son, which I did bear.

And the other woman said, Nay; but the living is my son, and the dead is thy son. And this said, No; but the dead is thy son, and the living is my son. Thus they spake before the king.

Then said the king, The one saith, This is my son that liveth, and thy son is the dead: and the other saith, Nay; but thy son is the dead, and my son is the living.

And the king said, Bring me a sword. And they brought a sword before the king.

And the king said, Divide the living child in two, and give half to the one, and half to the other.

Then spake the woman whose the living child was unto the king, for her bowels yearned upon her son, and she said, O my lord, give her the living child, and in no wise slay it. But the other said, Let it be neither mine nor thine, but divide it.

Then the king answered and said, Give her the living child, and in no wise slay it: she is the mother thereof.

I Kings, 3: 16–27

It is easier for a poor mother to feed nine children
than for nine children to feed a mother.

(German saying)

Hundreds of stars in the pretty sky
Hundreds of shells on the shore together
Hundreds of birds that go singing by
Hundreds of birds in the sunny weather.

George Cooper (in a book of 1917)

Hundreds of dewdrops to greet the dawn
Hundreds of bees in the purple clover;
Hundreds of butterflies on the lawn
But only one mother the wide world over.

Anonymous (in a book of 1937)

A BABY'S FEET

A baby's feet, like sea-shells pink,
Might tempt, should heaven see meet,
An angel's lips to kiss, we think,
A baby's feet.

Like rose-hued sea-flowers toward the heat
They stretch and spread and wink
Their ten soft buds that part and meet.

No flower-bells that expand and shrink
Gleam half so heavenly sweet,
As shine on life's untrodden brink
A baby's feet.

A. C. Swinburne

BABY'S SKIES

Would you know the baby's skies?
Baby's skies are mother's eyes.
Mother's eyes and smile together
Make the baby's pleasant weather.

Mother, keep your eyes from tears,
Keep your heart from foolish fears.
Keep your lips from dull complaining
Lest the baby thinks it's raining.

M. C. Bartlett

Children are what the mothers are.
No fondest father's fondest care
Can fashion so the infant heart
As those creative beams that dart
With all their hopes and fears, upon
The cradle of a sleeping son.

Walter Savage Landor

Thou art thy mother's glass, and she in thee
Calls back the lovely April of her prime . . .

William Shakespeare (Sonnet III)

Sons are the anchors of a mother's life . . .

Sophocles (Phaedra)

Who ran to help me when I fell,
And would some pretty story tell,
Or kiss the place to make it well?
My Mother.

Ann Taylor

12

There was a young man loved a maid
Who taunted him. "Are you afraid,"
She asked, "to bring to me today
Your mother's heart upon a tray?"

He went and slew his mother dead
Tore from her breast her heart so red
Then towards his lady-love he raced
But tripped and fell in all his haste.

As the heart rolled on the ground
It gave forth a plaintive sound.
And it spoke, in accents mild:
"Did you hurt yourself, my child?"

Jean Richepin

MY TRUST

A picture memory brings to me;
I look across the years and see
Myself beside my mother's knee.

I feel her gentle hand restrain
My selfish moods and know again
A child's blind sense of wrong and pain.

But wiser now, a man gray grown,
My childhood's needs are better known.
My mother's chastening love I own.

John Greenleaf Whittier

14

TO MY MOTHER

There was so much I meant to tell you
While dwelling in that distant land—
And yet I always knew full well, you
Would be the one to understand.

Now that I hold in reverend hand
At last an offering of my own
For you—as I had long since planned—
My first true gift: now you are gone.

Yet, strangely, as I read those lines
I feel my grief for you grow less
So soothingly throughout them shines
The radiance of your gentleness.

Hermann Hesse

God could not be everywhere; therefore he made mothers.

Arab Saying

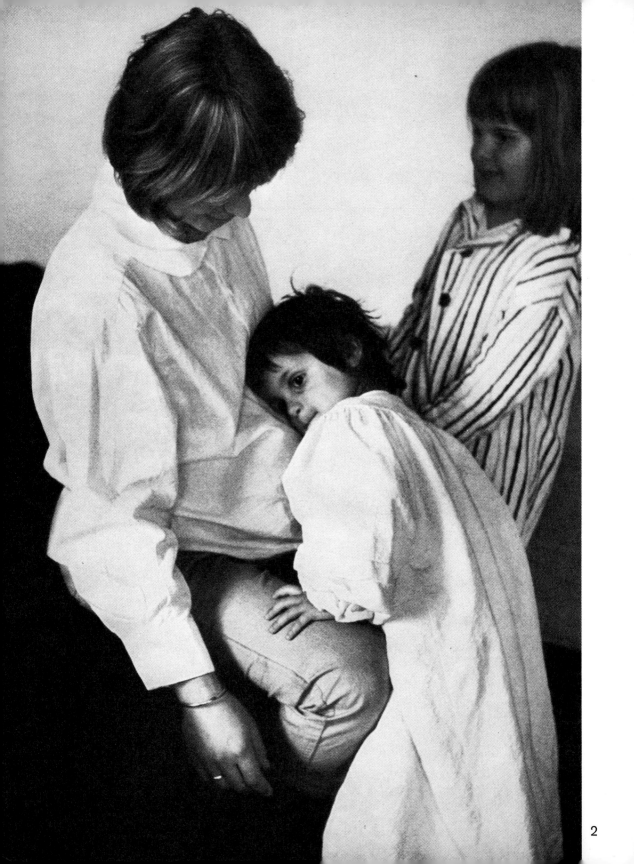

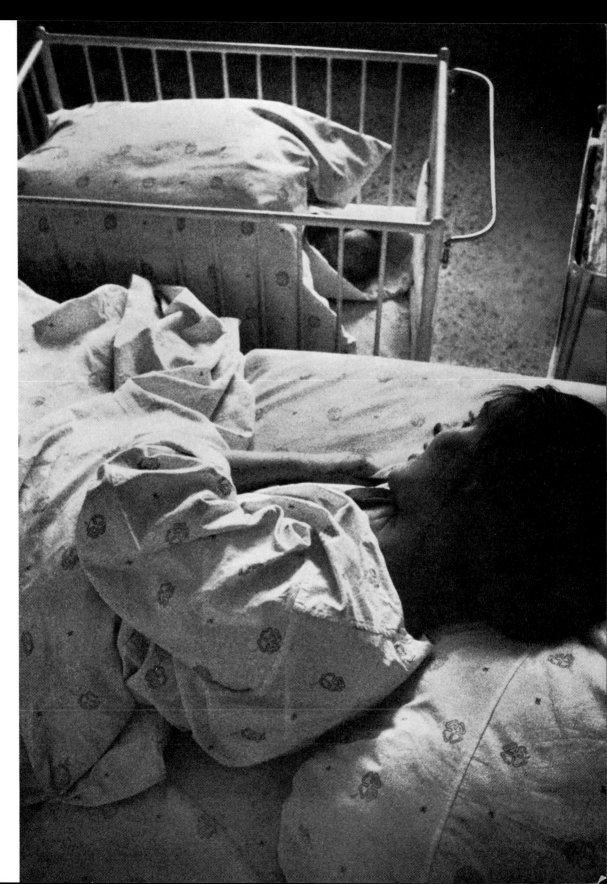

3

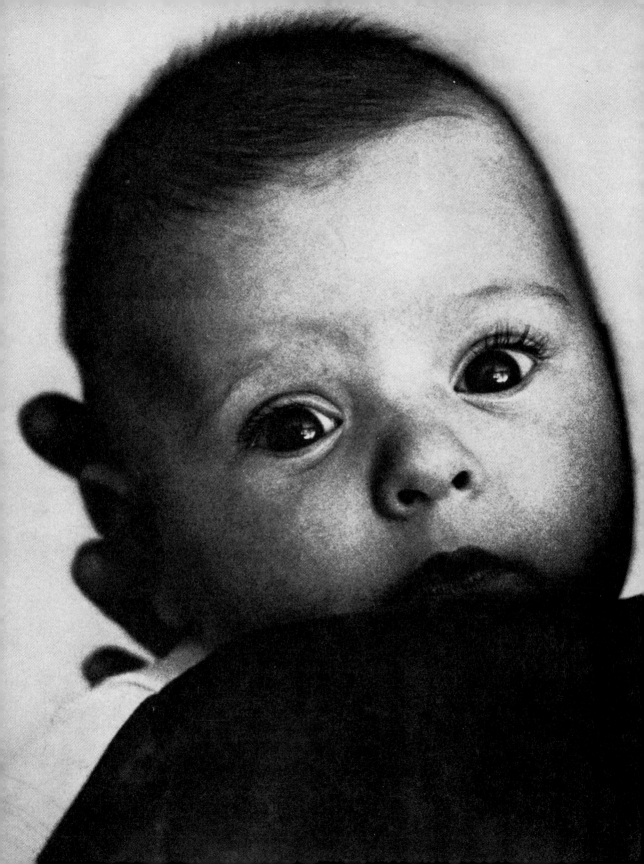

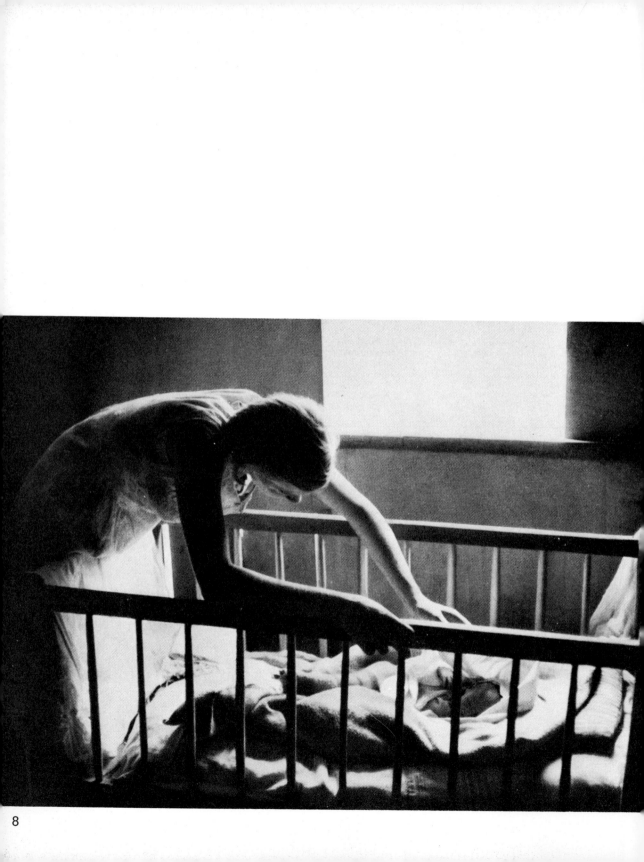

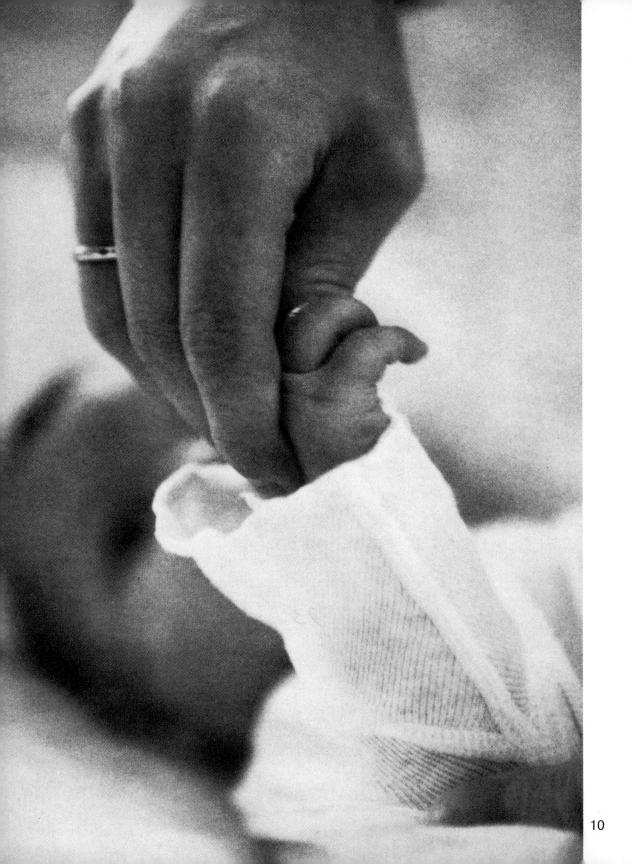

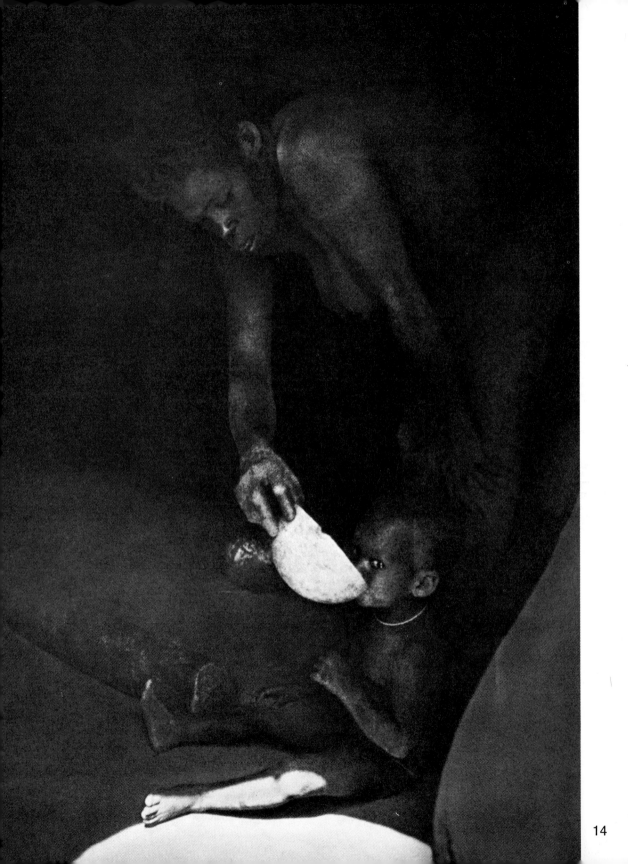

14

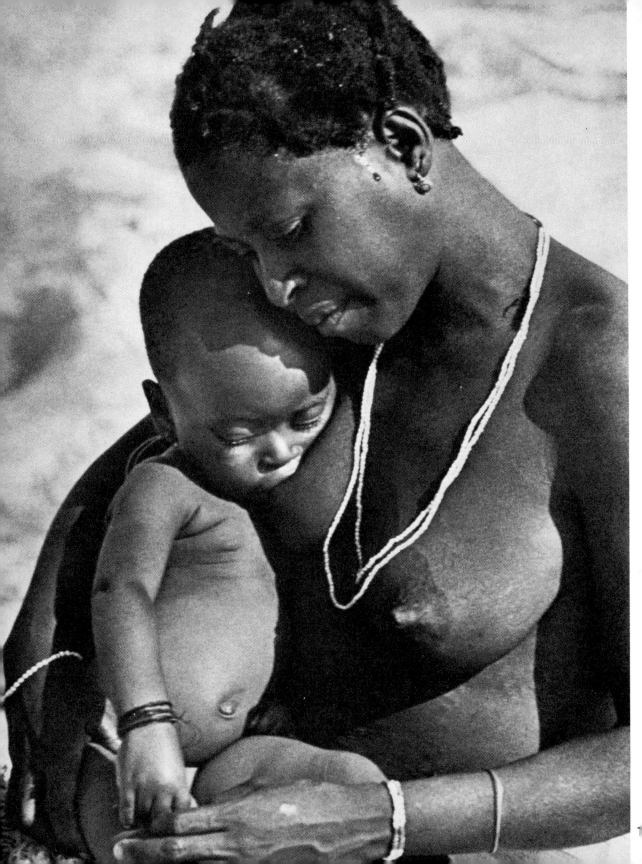

Sweet and low, sweet and low,
Wind of the western sea,
Low, low, breathe and blow,
Wind of the western sea!
Over the rolling waters go,
Come from the dying moon, and blow,
Blow him again to me;
While my little one, while my pretty one sleeps.

Sleep and rest, sleep and rest,
Father will come to thee soon;
Rest, rest, on mother's breast,
Father will come to thee soon;
Father will come to his babe in the nest,
Silver sails all out of the west
Under the silver moon;
Sleep, my little one, sleep, my pretty one, sleep.

Alfred Lord Tennyson

A mother's heart is a son's most beautiful and inalienable dwelling place, even after his hair has turned gray—and each of us has only *one* such heart in all the universe.

Adalbert Stifler

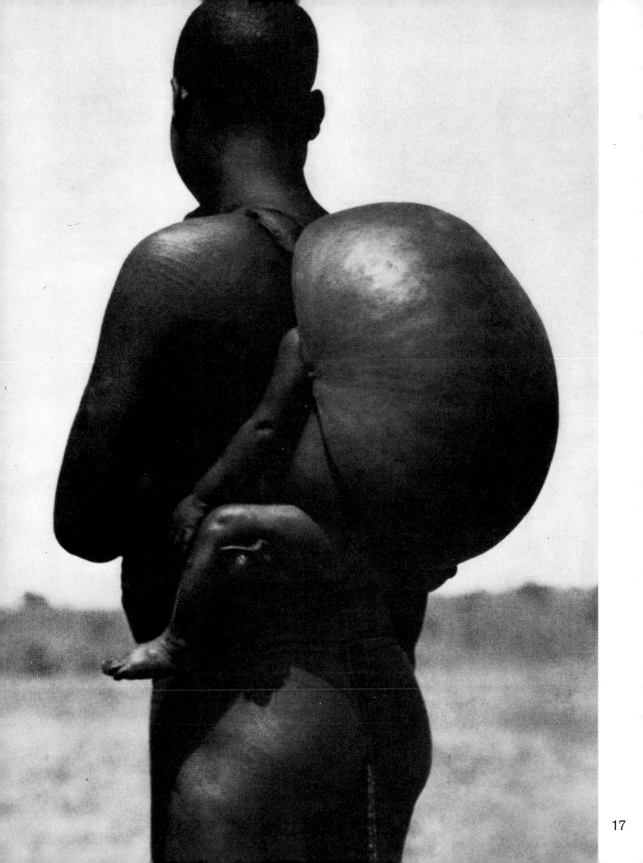

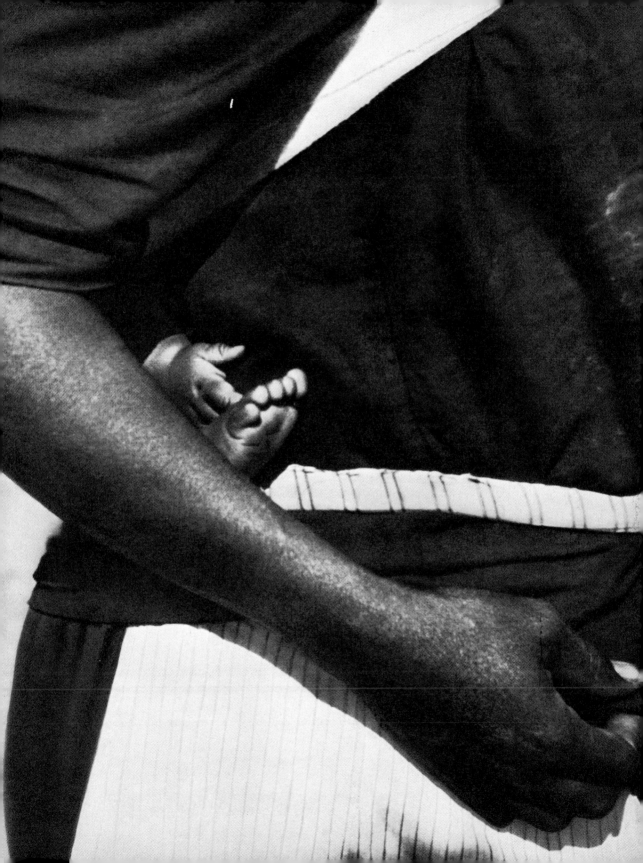

Nothing is more charming than to see a mother with a child in her arms, and nothing inspires greater reverence than a mother among many children.

Johann Wolfgang von Goethe

Mother is the name for God in the lips and hearts of little children.

William Makepeace Thackeray

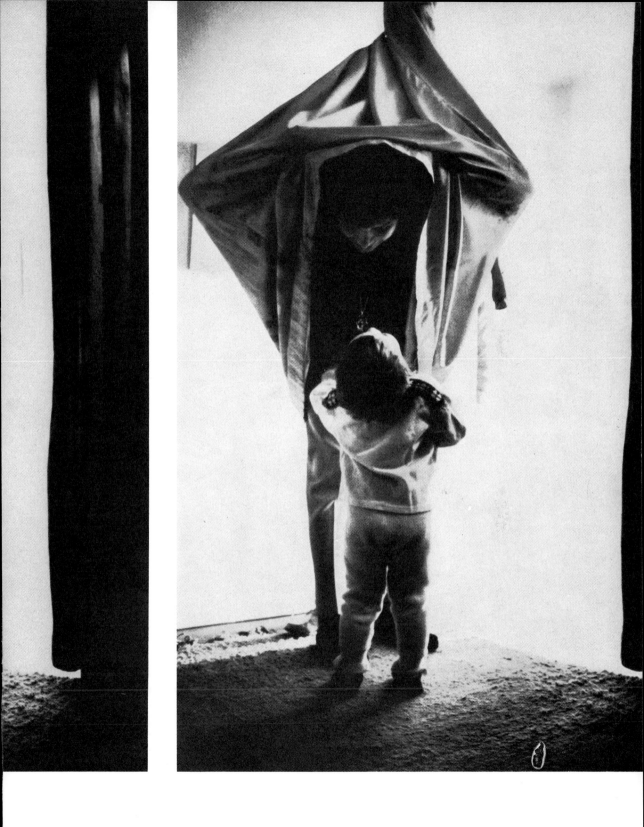

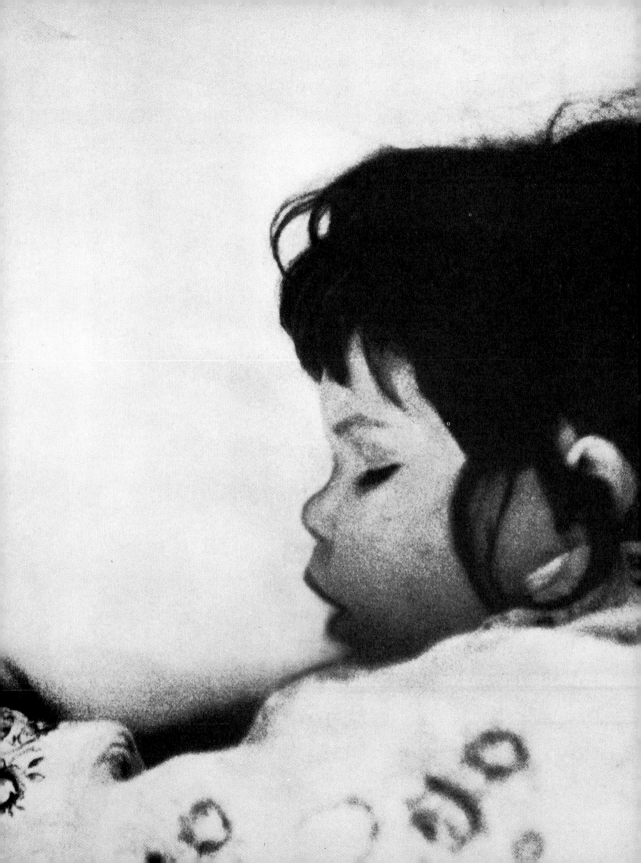

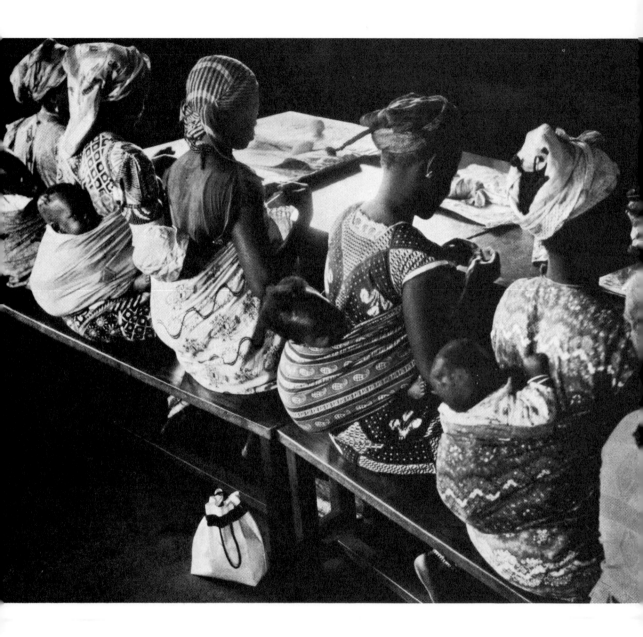

Heaven is at your mother's feet.

Persian Saying

We are born into life—it is sweet, it is strange.
We lie still on the knee of a mild Mystery
Which smiles with a change;
But we doubt not of changes, we know not of spaces,
The Heavens seem as near as our mother's face is,
And we think we could touch all the stars that we see;
And the milk of our mother is white on our mouth;
And, with small, childish, hands we are turning around
The apple of Life, which another has found—

Elizabeth Barrett Browning
(from A Rhapsody of Life's Progress)

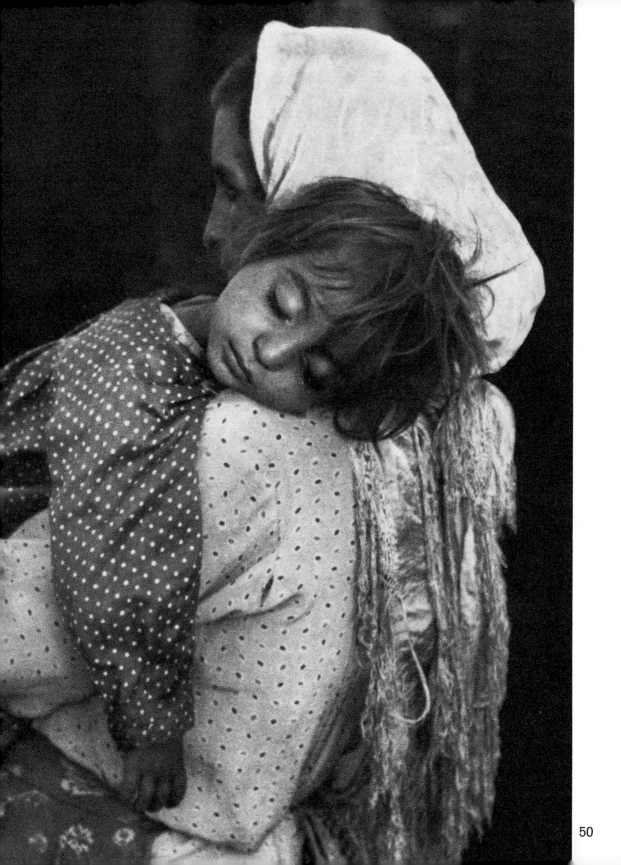

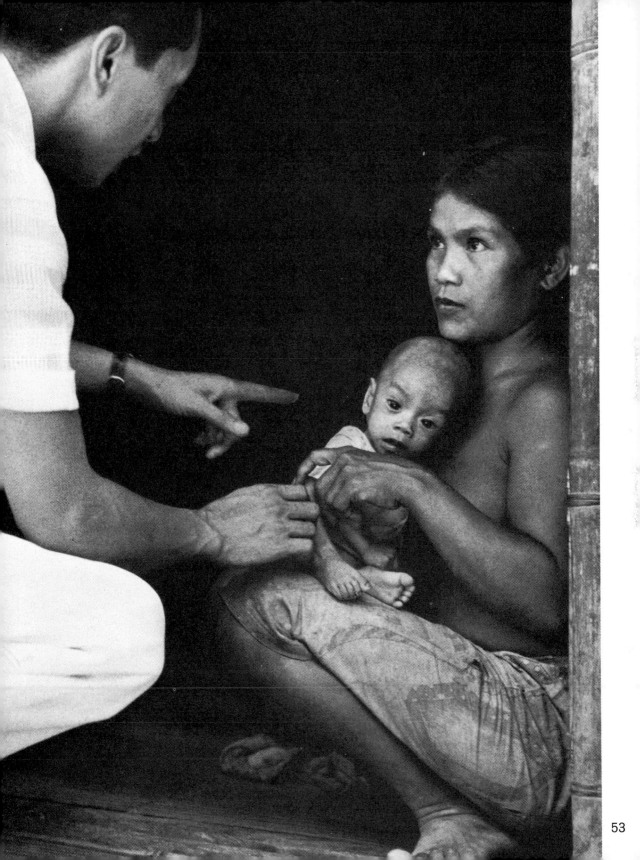

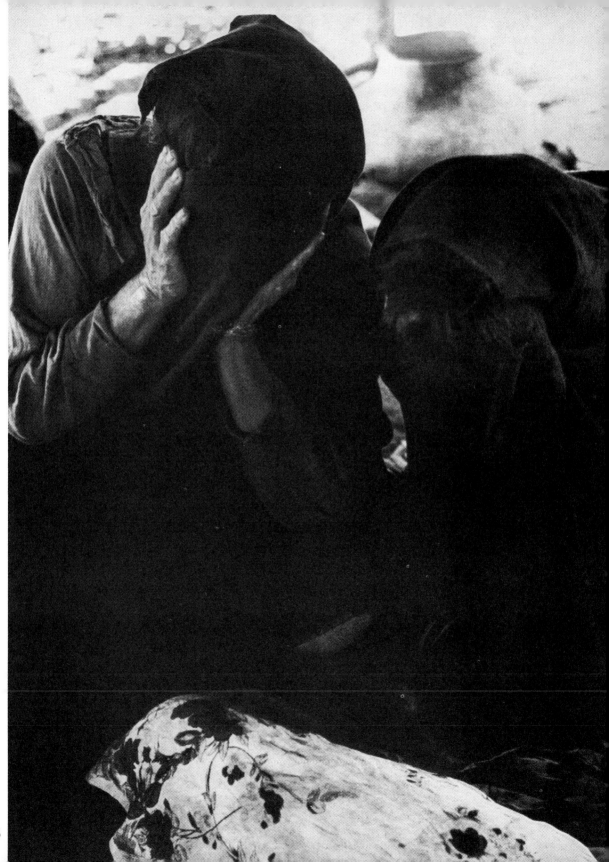

I feel that, in the heavens above,
The angels whispering to one another,
Can find among their burning terms of love
None so devotional as that of "Mother."

Edgar Allan Poe

He maketh the barren woman to keep house, and
to be the joyful mother of children.

Psalm 113: 9

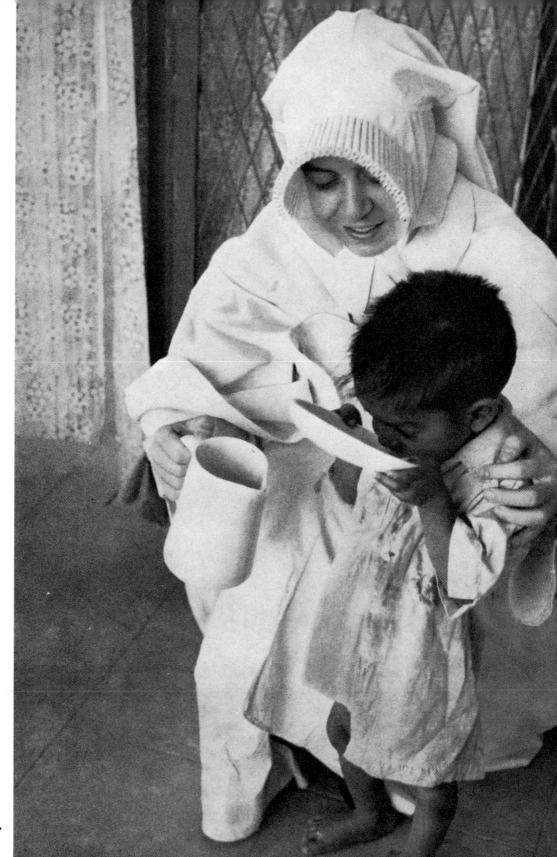

TABLE OF PHOTOGRAPHS

ACKNOWLEDGMENTS: Pictures 30, 55 and the back-cover picture are here reprinted by kind permission of Franckh'sche Verlagshandlung Stuttgart; the poem on page 13 is from *Mother and Child,* published by Migros-Genossenschafts-Bund, Zurich; the poem "To My Mother" from *Early Poems* by Hermann Hesse, G. Grothe'sche Verlagsbuchhandlung KG. Cologne and Berlin.